Amelia Earhart

by

Larry Beckett

Finishing Line Press
Georgetown, Kentucky

Amelia Earhart

Copyright © 2018 by Larry Beckett
ISBN 978-1-63534-635-0 First Edition
All rights reserved under International and Pan-American Copyright Conventions.
No part of this book may be reproduced in any manner whatsoever without written permission from the publisher, except in the case of brief quotations embodied in critical articles and reviews.

ACKNOWLEDGMENTS

Thanks are due to Laura Fletcher and Robin Rule for arranging the first performances of this poem.

Publisher: Leah Maines

Editor: Christen Kincaid

Cover Art: Cover photograph taken by Albert L. Bresnik
           Hollywood photographer to the stars and Amelia Earhart

Author Photo: Laura Fletcher

Cover Design: Elizabeth Maines McCleavy

Printed in the USA on acid-free paper.
Order online: www.finishinglinepress.com
           also available on amazon.com

Author inquiries and mail orders:
Finishing Line Press
P. O. Box 1626
Georgetown, Kentucky 40324
U. S. A.

Dreams call to me
over a rose-tinted sea:
I wait on the shore
for the one I adore.

When my dreamboat comes home,
then my dreams no more will roam:
I will meet you and I will greet you,
hold you closely, my own.

Moonlit waters will sing
of the tender love you bring:
we'll be sweethearts for ever
when my dreamboat comes home.

—Dave Franklin, 1936

relative peace in the Asia-Pacific region
but the chairman had concerns over ongoing
conflicts elsewhere. He urged the foreign
ministers, in Jakarta, yesterday, to sign
the nuclear test ban treaty before winter.
This is Radio Hong Kong, broadcasting on
short wave frequency 6210 mhz. It is now

blue midnight, and the Royal Observatory
reports 28° Celsius, and occasional gusts
offshore. The tropical blue storm Gloria,
over the western ocean, now moving north-
west, at 15 km/hr, is approaching blue
landfall. The blue weather's mainly fine,
apart blue from a few isolated showers.

Oh listen, the blue flight had no landing,
the worlds are out of balance, and because
the airplane vanished, I, never arriving,
now haunt the raw newspaper, and in words
I hate. Do you read me? in the white noise
tonight, unknown! in air, history, lost,
down here with the legends, sea serpent,

mermaid, I sprawl, unburied, by the wreck
Electra, withering in the salt, -3 miles
altitude, no navigator, as the fish knock
my ribs, and coral grows on my white bones,
unsleeping, in the lurid current, clouds
foam, in seaweed, in deep; in life, I flew
2 oceans, but ghosts can't cross water: oh

for the love of pity, listen, till morning
is here, and I go dead. Where on earth did

1

I end up, they wonder, on the next-to-last
jump of the '37 world flight? That question
leads to a cheap mythology... Cue violins,
as usual, for the Hollywood movie, in black-
and-white, romance, suspense, courage, in

this Pacific mystery, starring the glamour
girl aviator, torn between the navigator,
the love interest, and the good old U.S.A.,
in the dynamite story officials didn't dare
reveal before Pearl Harbor: she didn't fly
east, as announced, but north on a mission
for the military, diverted to the islands

mandated to the Rising Sun, and reporting
false positions to cover, overflying Truk
lagoon, low pass, by landing lights, air-
fields and shipyards, illegal, for a war.
The code word cloudy in her radio traffic
told Navy intelligence, surveillance had
the American fleet in danger of assault

by zeros. She hit bad weather; not able
to see Howland Island, in the salt haze,
with an off chart, and the voice channel
jammed, by the sabotage? of her own Coast
Guard, no directions, the other plan, fly
back and ditch in the forbidden islands,
the air-sea search giving the Navy, in

combing the ocean, reconnaissance, in 4
quadrants, by cutter, minesweeper, battle-
ship, 4 destroyers, aircraft carrier, and
all its airplanes, criss-crossing. Coming
in on empty, she crashed on an outlying
reef, across blue water from a low atoll,
her lover banging his head, oh but alive.

She was in the Red Cross, and bandaged him,

in the lifeboat, rowing over shallows, to
the beach, in no man's land, and burying
her maps and instruments under a palm tree;
fishermen, hiding in the jungle, caught
her eye, and motioning to them, she saw,
out of the grass huts, soldiers, hustling,

dark looks at the down airplane, questions
in bad English:—American spy girl? and her
man laughed, was slapped, she cried out hurt,
was waved at gunpoint to a seaplane. . . Cross
fade, to a long shot, caption, Garapan City,
Saipan; military police, cracking a joke:
—The U.S. has to use a woman under cover,

their men are cowards. . . They dragged him
away, hands tied, walked her, arms black
and blue, to a rain-streaked prison hotel,
iron bars in the useless windows, snails
crawling, her thumbs hung in metal rings
above her as she sagged against the wall.
The dysentery she caught in Java flared

up; they changed her out of her trousers
into a blue shift. The girl, looking after
her, smiled, handing her an apple, touched
her breast:—Consolacion; and she winced,
thanking her with a pearl ring. They shot
3 endings, and showed them to avg. people
to see what would go over at the box office.

Oh the crackpots who cash in on my enigma
and ride my name like a ghost automobile
down easy to the bank, hack into steaming
jungles, hunting for wreckage, interview
old South Sea islanders who squint at my
photo and nod, and who see in documents
declassified by the Navy, conspiracies:

like the suspicious Air Force major, retd.,
whose obsessions led him to Long Island,
the Sea Spray Inn, in '64, a meeting of
the Early Flyers, cocktails and memories,
and the mystery woman:—Ah, you knew AE?
Her eyes glimmering, she said very well,
no photographs, please; she had on her oak

leaf decoration and the red-white-and-blue
ribbon for the Atlantic flight:—You think
she's dead? She said she was alive as long
as we remember her. With his voice shaking:
—I know it's you, Amelia: you say you're
married, but if I write the Phoenix Islands
into a column, Gardner, Enderbury, Sydney,

Birnie, Phoenix, Hull, Canton, and McKean,
I can draw a circle through the letters
of your so-called husband's name, oh and
its positions, 1st, 7th, 2nd, etc., mean
172 ° 13' W longitude, 4° 21' S latitude,
at the very lagoon on Hull Island where
your plane went down: I cracked the code!

I know everything: that morning, you had
company: fighters off the Japanese carrier

looming in Jaluit harbor; the machine guns
rattled, and you tried to veer, your thin
aluminum belly ripped, black smoke blowing
out of you, bawled your line of position,
last message, and crash-landed on the edge

of the closest atoll, all the birds, foam
hissing, and the plane burning. You looked
at the buzzing sky, and the American flyer
on patrol, and waved to him, oh but before
your rescue, this landing boat shoved into
the blue lagoon, leaving the red sun flag;
they took you to jail in Saipan, questions,

to the Imperial Palace, in Tokyo: kept in
that luxury prison, U.S. hero under wraps,
in a kimono, you learned the tea ceremony,
under a master, taught language, and were
allowed to fly their sister to your world-
flight plane. 7 springs, and 7 blossomings
of the cherries. . . One night, in June '44,

you filled in on radio for demoralizing
Tokyo Rose, and not knowing it was to air
your voice as blackmail in a treaty, you
started out:—Ah, hello, all-forgetting
and forgotten blue Yankee veterans out
in the South Pacific, it's the Zero Hour,
for boys with time to kill. Okay, on old

timer's night, it's—hold on, flash: After
4 days of bombing and off-shore shelling,
a U.S. force has now gained the beachhead
at Saipan—hurrah for Main St., brass bands
on Independence Day! And you played Stars
and Stripes Forever, till the secret police
raided the station, cut off the broadcast,

and put you under arrest in a blind house.

It had backfired; America abandoned you
under the rose of secrecy. Surrender day,
on 1 condition, the emperor not be given
to the Allies and hung, they let you go.
1st woman ashore, off of a B-29, to pick
up pows, your old comrade, Jackie Cochran:

she'd come to spirit you, older, heavier,
incognito in a nun's white veil, not back
to that publicity inferno, your ballyhoo
husband, and his 1-upmanship, but to a new
life, and in the perfect disguise, a dress,
and makeup, with your hair done, legally
dead, and living on in Bedford Hills. Etc.

Ah, the dead are vulnerable, who can't
impeach the forgeries of the definitive
bio, which won't come out till publishers
hear what new slant the author can give
to the old life to sell it again, whether
I was my husband's act, or a bad flyer,
by word of them I let down or beat out,

and add acknowledgements, prologue, cold
facts, photographs, epilogue, appendices,
glossary, notes, reading, index, and maps
on the end papers, quotes from the reviews
on the slick jacket. She had to time it,
drop her ailerons, slide over the blank
ocean, guess altitude or else, and stall:

after the roar all night, oh grace, if only
a minute, and silence, bang down on the hard
water, pitching forward, white wash, cockpit
hauled under by the engines, and no way out
by hatch, the zero tanks floating the tail,
and the listing airplane, lifting, sagging,
in the rough waves,—Ah Christ, she saw,

we're sinking; the sea poured into vents,
flooding across her feet, no time, and no
Jacob's ladder, she had to climb on out,
up the catwalk, hand hold, on the radio,
jam boots against gas tanks, backsliding,
but she got to the navigator, blood down
his face, he'd hit the table, star-crossed,

with 2 highway smash-ups before the flight,
and his new bride, no answer, he was knocked

out, and working to the life raft, she yanked
it, looked out the window at the deep ocean,
right there, inflating it to 1/2, she sighed
and then leaned out, lugging it out the door,
the day so bright, wrestling the man into it,

pumping it full, and tethering it, she
went back for compass, matches, canteen,
kite, ax, no flares, left back, and to
the awful door, he was slipping under
the water, no hope, the raft sinking, oh
and his loose arm flying out as a shark
rammed him, more following, all failing,

no way to swim, this hit parade song going
in her head, she felt—I don't want to be
Ophelia, pulled beneath "from her melodious
lay to muddy death;" no warning, and over-
whelmed by water, the airplane went down
and her with it, chaos swallowing, waves
closing above her, she held her breath

and breathed, salt water cut her throat,
life flashed: daddy's fish story the 1st
airplane state fair that peach basket hat
bound for the port of nowhere yearbook
the curse at Kalamazoo River no swimming
and she fly by feel and I you mean seat
of the pants the rudder vibrating I'm

the organ grinder is my lost jackknife in
the moon and tall headline Boston woman
flies into morning on surprise Horseshoe
Bend big train I'm dancing on the firebox
in dirty overalls Lucky Strike ad and I
don't smoke fast woman they hiss no hats
Gyp says out the strange door into this

green sea publicity dive and I fly in as

maid of honor canaries 1 ocean I hate
to get my hair wet the showgirls cancan
on the wings movie the mansion on fire
2 oceans the bear went over the mountain
to gulf dear cowboys point cheap lawyer
pilots are always dreaming to California

by the long way the code keys and trailing
antenna useless morning sick am I pregnant
lost star Electra of the Pleiades and there
are always islands, drowning, hand, air—Oh,
ball up the pages of those phantom stories,
and throw them out; all wrong: they hurt
my ghost. And I go back to my transmission.

The summer is harsh, this island morning,
the load heavy in our Lockheed: I cock
to the engine's rhythm, keep wondering
if the fuel flow is okay, flight check,
lift finger Ready, gun and idle, stick
under my palm, I sigh and grin, wave at
the colonists and natives, and roll out

of the aerodrome, swing, taxi, gun twice,
open her, 1000 yards, all dirt, and rough,
she won't pull up, 50 to the cliff, cross-
road bounces me, into the air, and off,
green ocean, as I sink down, light surf,
see bottom, at my shadow, the fish scatter
like fireworks, 6 feet, I spray up water

and start to climb, the clouds, 100 feet,
ah! goodbye, New Guinea. . . Dreams call
to me. Noonan, in back; we're on our next-
to-last leg, to the coral island, middle
of nowhere, by dead reckoning, radio coil,
star sextant. . . over a rose-color sea. . .
How many fathoms down does our mother go?

As little sister, who I call blue pigeon,
after the song, and I'd say, oh thousands
of years ago, when mama was young, June,
1890, her presentation ball, pine boards
in a back yard pavilion, Japanese lanterns
in the garden, dusk, St. Joe men playing
slow waltzes and reels, she was greeting

and in walked daddy: she liked him and saw
he liked her. 7 years after, ah thousands

of years ago, in summer, I was born, Amelia,
her mama, Mary, his, Earhart, the judge's
granddaughter, in Atchison; but daddy was
a railroad man: I'm from there, Kansas City,
Des Moines, St. Paul, Springfield, Chicago,

and down the line. . . in a gold rush water
hole, on Quality Hill, in grandma's house:
her ma saw George Washington riding a mare,
and she her daughter in an airplane: this
flying country. My birthdays, all picnics,
no party, no dress, and I can whoop it up
in the green woods, go wild, and only slip

home for July 24 ice cream, in the mixer. . .
I'm a jayhawk and go stilt walking, I whiz
till the swing jumps, go for a whirl on our
flying dutchman, and ride it till she dies,
upside down, the tomboy, and so mama folds
our frills away; skirts are fragile, and you
are dressed in caution; Aunt Maggie sews blue

bloomers, tucked at the knee, invented by
Amelia Bloomer, for freedom of legs: the 1st
in town, I go, loose and outcast, Saturday
indian, in disguise, with daddy, who taught
me to waltz, that wonder, and then I put
on Alexander's Ragtime Band and dance, la!
to the Red Wing on the wind-up Victrola.

Our big dog has the tease boys on the roof,
and turns on me, roiling: I remember daddy:
—Don't ever run;—Oh James Ferocious you've
tipped your water again; I out my hand to
his hackles, lead him in the kitchen. Daddy:
—You were brave with him.—Oh I never had
time to be scared. He kissed my forehead.

St. Louis, World's Fair, 1904, I pleaded

to go on sky cars, mama said no; I rode
the elephant, the ferris wheel, and tried
to make a roller coaster in our back yard.
Uncle Nicey anchors wood to the roof stud,
long nails, 8 feet high, slaps it:—Good;
I shin up with a skate wheel board I made:

—Let me go; I slide down, track greased,
and bang a trestle, crack up; shirt torn,
and my lip bloody:—Oh Pidge, it's just
like flying! Mama had Sadie tear it down,
but daddy, who let us stay up to gaze on
the comet, Xmas gave me a boy's sled that
I could bellyflop on, would've okayed it.

I see the water rising, Missouri in flood,
on the way home, slopping over the tracks,
logs slamming the coach, oil lamps dead,
river snarling, train inching, bad leaks:
—As long as the fire's going, it works,
says daddy. Pigeon:—You afraid, Meelie?
—Course not. . . Exploring, we go through

our orchard, of apples, peaches, and plums,
under a ditch at the back fence, to danger,
in the thorns, with badgers for buffaloes,
the outlaw cave, ashes, bottles, old paper,
for treasure, big whirls in the yellow river,
the banks washing out, the climb back hard,
late for supper, and the bluff is outlawed.

That summer night, crickets going, locusts
saying It's hot, the bluejays quiet, bats
skittering, at dusk, the sun a ball of peace
under off-color clouds, above the tall grass,
fireflies, odors out of the white hollyhocks,
rose geraniums, dark heliotropes; we traipse
out of the arbor, holding a snatch of grapes:

grandma:—Quit that racing in the garden;
I'm hot just looking: on the verandah, girls.
I, on imagination's horse:—Whoa, Saladin;
but grandma, when we go quick the air blows
on us, to cool; and she throws up her hands.
Toot and Katch call from next door:—Cousins!
and she nods:—Go through the gate, ladies.

I jump the fence, as always. She drawls:—I
never used to do all that, only roll hoops. . .
The 2nd St. arc light comes on, and Charlie
carries a taper to our soft North Terrace
gas light; time to go in, for boys' success
stories: Onward & Upward, Through by Day,
The Starry Flag; no dolls, only my donkey,

Donk, who walks in puddles, hammers nails,
and comes to bed. It was going to last
for honeymoons to come; one morning it was
all whisked away. Good night, gas light,
horse & carriage, old century, good night,
grandma's house, good night, childhood.
It's quarter to, time to radio the ground.

KHAQQ TO LAE AT 8000 FEET SIGNS OF STRONGER-
THAN-FORECAST HEADWINDS

Because daddy, my 1st word, who made days
adventures, in big vocabulary, with his
mystery inventions, challenges, our arias
at the upright piano, riding to parties,
1 dance and back at midnight, one fall was
off the streetcar, and balance, no spring
in his walk, no larking, and saying nothing

to mama's ice look; he was in the hotel bar
with railroad men, and couldn't hold booze.
And it was letdowns, black moods, the cure,
firings, other cities. I was packing his
bag for a Great Northern run, and there's
a flask; I empty it in the sink; he barks
and is about to slap me, when mama stops

his arm. He never. . . Because I was hissed
weak sister at high school, for not fooling
around behind the deaf teacher, atheist
at boarding school, for not bible pounding
that indian poet; why have you-be-damning
girls' clubs, and why must Ghosts be taboo?
and the headmistress blazed. In chemistry,

on a hard question, I just quote poetry:
"autour de premier aeroplane," circles
Apollinaire, in air. . . In carriage, ah,
I'm a hockey star, and I hate the graces:
walk so, bow so, my law! the exercises:
big room, with a little chair, you aim
your behind and climb on; it's a scream. . .

What animal display is it that a woman old
enough to breed must be glamorized? Hair
only to comb and curl, eyebrows pluck and
pencil, eyes shadow, line, lashes mascara,
skin, pancake, cheeks, rouge, nose, powder,
lips, red grease, ears hole, hoop, throat
circle, perfume, breasts bra, waist corset,

wrists bracelet, ring finger ring, nails
gloss, hips girdle, legs shave, hose, heels
high, rig out in silks, frills, feathers,
chains, and never age, your image? I was
made by god, good to the world's 7 seas,
and I don't need makeup: oh my bare body
is actual divinity. Amen; it's in the eye.

I went after the pigeon to Canada, lolling
by the glass lake, trying to play the New
World Symphony on the banjo, and studying
auto mechanics with boys. . . Because I saw
3 one-legged men, King St., at Xmas, who
were back from the Great War, which wasn't
brass bands, dancing with uniforms; I quit

school for the Red Cross: 12 on, 2 off, at
the new Military Hospital, cooking, washing,
for the paralyzed g.i.s, oh the shell shocked;
when it's a fire alarm, I hear them howling,
begging. At the Armistice, whistles blowing,
inaudible speeches, music, streamers flying,
hullabaloo, and not 1 word of thanksgiving.

It's a man's game, but let's open up honor:
draft women, so they can blind, burn, gun
down, murder, suffer, shovel the dead under,
die in headlines; don't give me that line
about chivalry, their frailty; bull: women
do so much of the dirt work in the world,
nobody looks. Let them in the foxhole, and

men will clear out; we'll be done with wars,
I told the Daughters of the American Rev.
Ah! "Damned spirits all, that in crossways
and floods have burial." Crossroad, ocean.
—I'll go west, keep mama married, Pigeon:
after, it's my life. You wait on the shore.
Look at those clouds. . . Oh the one I adore.

I'm coming into them, in the forecast,
Pearl Harbor wireless, but I can go
over the rain squalls, 250 miles east
of the island, it's a pleasure, to 10K
for now. Stick back, ease into it, on my
own, give her throttle: how many horses
under the cowling? I rode on Saturdays

at the Toronto stables, and saw that big
and rawboned dapple gray.—Hey March, ah can
I ride him?—That outlaw? Can you get a leg
over him? I guess his old cavalry man
was mean: Dynamite, bucking for the moon,
throwed 2 boys lately, kicking like hell.
I split my apple, and step to his stall:

his ears go back, he shows his teeth—Ts, ts;
I lay the green crescents in with his feed,
and palm his neck: like when I had to balance
on a wood crate, at the tiny window, the shed
next door, the pretty mare, all cramped inside,
heat, flies; she'd bang her hoofs, and the man
would whip her, hard to break her; I'd reach in

grass and caresses, and she'd calm. That black
beauty, one day, spooks at a newspaper blowing
and shies, he lashes her, she flinches, her tack
comes loose, and Nellie bolts, her traces flying,
down the drive, and—Runaway! he's yelling;
did the angel of the wild say jump? and she
is off the bridge, oh, if only she could fly,

and cracks into the thin waters, Kaw River.
—Mr. Oldham twisted his ankle, dear, would

you take a piece of Sadie's cake on over.
I move my hands behind my back; I stand,
shaking my head: no. I was all of 7, and
till then I'd never disobeyed my mama. Oh
to get my heels off of the ground: I'd go

from curb to shafts, and crawl up on the fat
heavy-footed sorrel at the butcher's wagon,
who'd warp his backbone for nothing.—Lift
me down, mama. . . Give me a horse of my own,
grandma!—Don't want you riding, little woman.
—Why?—Because I say so. It's the same hiss
as for mama, who did tricks on a circus horse

behind her back. We'd go live with the post-
man at, what was it, Minnesota lake, summers,
help with haying; I'd get to take Prince out,
indian pony, with a white star on his nose,
who got away with dawdling, and my bare heels
on his big flanks won't urge him. In hopes,
I flirt his reins, lope to a fence, he leaps

over and down, spraying up mud: ah love,
he's snickering from hunger; no saddle,
and I walk back, after. We were both 12;
I'd brush him out, and he'd nuzzle my little
shoulder, spirit him sugar, and he'd gentle.
Like with Dynamite, who I fed every night
on my way home, and in a month, he'd hit

a canter; I handled him, with an easy bit
and my light hands.—March, what do I owe?
—Nothing; you saved him, Amelia. Pilot,
the Royal Flying Corps:—Hey, I like how
you ride him, in reflex; you have to play
it, like my aeroplane; it goes like silk;
and if it's contrary, you have a comeback.

Come out to Armour Heights next week and see.

He's like the Hospital boys:—It's flying, is
all; if you crash, you crash: I ain't a hero.
—Okay; can I go up, etc.?—Ah, no civilians.
His snow lashes me; he clears the evergreens,
circles over the fair grounds: in my 20 eye,
the little plane, dark against the winter sky,

harsh sun, red wings, the ace: and he dives at
my sister and I, watching on a grassy clearing,
jazzing us because we're girls: if he loses it,
we're goners, and she lights out; daddy's strong
—Don't ever run; I stand: what is it saying,
that red aeroplane, as it rushes over my head?
All my free hours after are at the airfield:

airspeed down, foot the right rudder, holding
against the torque, I jump it up, heels, oh!
in the air, on the cloud's bare back, riding,
rain slanting into the archipelago below,
on the landlubbers, under the gray sky, who
don't remember: above that ceiling of mist,
in this blue world, the sun is always out.

I can straight-and-level at this altitude,
stick force on my hand zero, and it flies
itself, better than I, when there's no need;
steady it, and not by the cant of the nose,
but by wings and horizon: counterclockwise
around the world, nothing to do but conjure. . .
I stuck a feather from the turkey duster

into the turned up brim of my straw hat
like a rough rider for my easter bonnet
as I made do, when daddy, off a street-
car, drunk, was in a St. Paul accident,
our last $10 going to stitch up his cut.
Oh and the electric streetcar rides I had
in L.A., early 20s, 4th St. to the end

of the line, by the ho-hum buildings,
to my flying lessons, where I can sit
in a sphere of air, freedom, all vectors
open to me: and in my pilot's helmet,
leather jacket I sleep in to age it,
breeches and boots, ah! the looks I get:
am I a freak? I hide in the Rubaiyat,

"And naked on the Air of Heaven ride."
I was behind the ropes, at the air show:
—Is he the host, daddy, ask him what kind
of money to learn; I'd sneak under, but I
can't have him laughing at outlandish me.
—$100/hr, 10 hrs. Why are you so curious?
—I want to fly. And I went up with Hawks,

that barnstormer, 1 buck for 10 minutes,
in his old war surplus crate, and I mean

it's wired together.—My $. Who's this?
—He's flying with us.—Ah; why? They grin
till I catch on: they think I'm a woman
and frail, I might crack up, into hysteria,
jump, oh and the man's there to be my hero:

—I've been around aeroplanes, and I'm cool;
—Sorry, lady, if he don't go, you don't.
1st flight, white morning, and this fool
man babysitting me, crammed in the front
cockpit; air clear, the motor loud, we lift
over the oil derricks, the orange groves,
downtown, to where the Hollywood Hills

and the blue Pacific, strangers, now are
side-by-side in my eye; I see an island
shining out there; he idles, smooth air,
mocking me,—20000 feet! we're at 300;
my soul and body, lilting to fly, oh and
over the world's edge. At supper,—Holy
smoke, ah you're not daydreaming, Millie?

I can't afford that. I worked, for $1/hr,
horsed with the mail room boys, was snubbed
by the society girls, squeal! this is where
I get off and walk, down Long Beach Blvd.
Men run the show, join the service, get paid
to learn; the controls, even the parachute,
fit their bodies, and we have to make shift,

and I paid Neta, that he-woman, red hair,
black flying coat, $1/minute with inherited
Liberty bonds, because she wouldn't sneer,
or scare me off. 1st, lectures on the ground,
in the tool shack, tin roof, santanna wind,
the day electric:—Air speed, gyro horizon,
altimeter, turn & bank. Go over the biplane.

—Okay: the cockpit, fuselage, wheel, strut,

static opening, engine, propeller, cool holes,
carb intake screen, oil radiator, wheel, strut,
wing, ailerons, flaps, stabilizers, elevators,
rudder, tail skid, and wing.—The aeroplane's
awkward on the ground: it lurches, and it
lags; but in the air, it's in its element.

By the oil wells, I hitch in a tin lizzy;
the little girl:—Why're you in those togs?
—I'm a flyer.—Oh that's dreamy, but you
don't look it, in braids. They cut mama's
long fox hair, 16: typhoid, superstitions
it weakened her; I pin mine up and back
so she can't tell I bob inches off week

by week: if I look female, they won't rag
at my aviating. I'm at Tweedy Road; today
I solo. In trousers, it's easier to leg
up into the aeroplane. I taxi, and blow
dust clouds; the left wing sags, and I
get out, fix the shock absorber, take off
and coil up over South Gate in the rough

air of beauty, to 5K, and so what, fooling,
loop, roll, and for the fun of it, like mama,
1st woman to go up Pike's Peak, sun breaking
down the gray sky, that morning, my soul, oh
flying, without a sex, alone, no saying no,
off earth, "can fling the Dust," and glory
with doves and swallows. I sideslip down to

telegraph poles, can I split them? I was 10,
coasting a hill, lying on that sled too tough
for girls, and out of nowhere, the junk man,
his horse, in front: too icy to turn, and deaf
to hear; I make up my mind, and slide in safe,
between the legs, under the horse, good thing
I was riding like a boy, and I whiz and bang,

bad landing, tail high, on the dry field.
This cornhusker takes a snapshot; the boys:
—Were you scared?—I sang, 1st time, loud
as I could.—Only thing you did right was
land it wrong; how was it? Neta:—Congrats,
AE!—Oh, nothing special, I say; but I'm
mile high, and I vow to save every dime

for that aeroplane; I overhear them call me
a natural, whoa! I'm sorry, Noonan, not here,
but daydreaming, wing low, the weight of my
arm on the stick, and so holding left rudder,
not thinking, going down, with back pressure,
right aileron, up elevator, when I should be
doing nothing, only feel it, and let her fly.

Oh I adore that moment, I launch into
the blue: 1 of 12 women flyers on earth, I
rounded up all my savings, help from mama
and even the pigeon, top $, for that new
air-cooled 3-cylinder 60-hp loud yellow
Canary, light and simple, and my 1st love,
out there on the apron, on my birthday 25.

They all call it a kite, but it's my own
sweet property, to air or crash, and I
can haul it by the tail, without a man.
It's a sandpiper, and it loves to fly:
mornings, I taxi it to the dirt runway,
and 3 points down, I eye an orange tree
at the other end; I throttle it up slow

to full, right rudder, to counter the torque,
go for that tree, the tail will come up when
it's good and ready, lift forward, don't walk
it, as the nose sways, tail up, I'm airborne,
controls go firm, stick back, ah ah, come on,
it gets light and skips, give it more angle
of attack, oh up, and I lark, wings level,

rev it, that roar an anthem, the arrow
to climb, I relax back, in this machine,
over the orange tree, in the open sky,
and do the impossible: I sit in heaven,
alive! tilting my wings. October, in
indirect sun, at the field, to advertise
the plane, I spiralled up, 1 hr, high as

she'll go; at 12K, she starts in knocking,
ah shoot, I'm climbing at a ft/sec, better

pull out. I land, saying,—What's wrong?
to the grease boys:—Spark control lever;
but look at this: the world's record for
ah, woman's altitude! 14K. I worked my way
up. Neta got hitched, and kissed it off; I

signed up with a joyrider, this army pilot,
after the war, never drifted out of flying,
the industry's backbone. I learned to stunt:
bank, skid, slip, spin, get out of anything,
loop, barrel roll, dare, in the beginning,
when the teacher had a crowbar to whack
you loose if your hand froze on the stick.

Ah, bless Bernouilli's principle: I fly
when lift = gravity, thrust drag; I rock
in the slipstream, and the propellers go
clockwise; I yaw and rudder, wind wake
scalloping clouds; and, power up, I break
into a characteristic stall, like a wave
falling, let go all controls: it'll dive

and recover to level, by itself—made, oh
to fly! ". . . Dorothy found she was riding"
a cyclone. That Kansas girl: this is my way
to Oz. I walk into the hangar, whistling,
blue salesman, for space, and interrupting
off-color jokes; I like to get all dirty,
studying with men, not in the air, wary

of inviting them, and their misgivings. At
the Air Rodeo:—You race?—I guess I can. . .
—Oh, he'll do the flying, you just ghost it,
and land, the lady winner.—No. Clouds blown,
jagging, in the blue grace, the coiling plane
over the congregation. I see the Milky Way,
wish I had time to make words dance for me;

I write, sign it Emil A. Harte: The hills

can't see the sun go down steeping the lake
they hold like I, from an airplane. Nichols
topped me, so I greased up my face and took
off, in my ship: the mackerel clouds prick
me, blank my goggles, no direction, sleet
on the light cotton wings, nothing for it

but to spin out of the snow, at 12K, shoot,
and quick—am I upside down? in a circle?
so long, break cloud, oh god, kick out
of it, landing, scared:—This vertical:
you go to sleep, sweetheart?—Ah no, I tail-
spun out, to get under the weather.—What
if it had lasted all the way?—Well, Hamlet

would make a bad pilot, with 2nd thoughts. . .
Landing is a power-off stall, all looking
for the gravity outlaw, in over the roofs,
low, on the approach, to get what's coming.
I scan out ahead, wing on line with wing,
holding out till no play in the elevators,
or travel in the stick, and touch 3 wheels

to earth. 1 bounce and they call it a crash:
I practise in secret. Mama left daddy, moving
back east, and I had to let it go for cash,
my Canary, to that air force kid, showboating
from the gas station to the light pole, doing
eights in a vertical bank, and oh sickening
look, slips off, down sideways, crumpling

into his graveyard. . . I was in the N.Y. Times
in my flying suit; cousins:—It's beneath us:
a lady's in print when she's born, marries,
and is buried. Oh fiddlesticks! They're ghosts
and don't know it. Cloud billows, tall banks,
I'm in the thick, better slide under, turn on
carb heat, and idle, and here she goes, down.

KHAQQ TO LAE AT 10000 FEET BUT REDUCING
ALTITUDE BECAUSE OF BANKS OF CUMULUS

I bought a car, the Yellow Peril, common
in L.A., bold in Boston, and drove across
the great divide. I had the old infection
that hurt flying, 24-hr sinus headaches;
they operated, and I took a pre-med course,
no doctor, but it woke up 5 years' memory,
green walks, and actual days, at Columbia:

I went everywhere forbidden, after class,
labyrinth of tunnels, the golden statue's
lap, and the library dome: I looked across
at the angel trumpeting above St. John's.
—Louise, the camera! In my button shoes,
long skirt, and black straw hat.—The pass-
key, Amelia, how'd you—I told him it's

in the name of science. He tried to razz
me, about a suicide jump. Look around us,
oh la! 100 cities in 1, electricity, jazz,
you'd have to be out of your mind to kiss
it off, in the daffodil spring, all this.
I knew that girl, with everything, once,
who cut her wrists out of a bad romance;

I sure enough don't know a man I'd die for.
—Well, last night, he proposed. —Ah Louise!
—Should I, I still have this year, 4 more
till my medical degree.—He has good eyes,
but why let your life go while he keeps his?
Your life.—Everyone is having babies but
me, and I, ah, maybe nobody else—So what?

It's worse to be on reins. Says I, who's not
in love. . . Let's go ride horses in the Park.

In 1920, when women in America got to vote.
Today, she's a doctor. Old roaring New York. . .
Years later, Sam asked me at a Boston quick-
lunch stand:—We have the fair play meetings,
swimming and tennis, the theater and kisses,

in common; honey, you ought to settle down
with me, come live in the Marblehead mansion.
—I love you, but no.—Why? my job at Edison,
my hours? I'll change companies, profession,
whatever.—You don't get it. I'm moving in
the House to work with kids, and I'm going
ahead, married or not: I might go flying.

—It's absurd; I'm the money maker.—I won't
be a housewife, okay? Stay in the kitchen
till I'm no good for anything outside it,
while the man dreams big. What is a woman?
Not second, out of Adam's rib: I have my own
backbone. You write a part that I won't play:
to be and not to do; I write myself. . . You

know what tore it?—No, what.—You were glad
I sold my airplane. All afternoon, the rains.
At the settlement house, in the back yard,
that April day, I was rehearsing the kids,
Through the Looking Glass, where Alice goes;
out of the blue, it's the telephone, for me:
—Miss Earhart, we wonder if you would do

something aeronautical and, well, dangerous?
—Is this a joke?—It's hush-hush.—Are you
a bootlegger?—You have a pilot's license?
Will you promise not to repeat what I—Okay.
—Would you like to fly the Atlantic?—Yeah.
At the interview, not 1 question on flying,
just the 3 men looking at my image, judging

my walk, my words. . . Mrs. Guest was the angel:

she bought the 3-motor monoplane from Byrd.
Her boy:—If you go, mother, I'll quit school;
—Get an American woman to do it, she said.
I wasn't too interesting to drown, was made
commander, and I'd pilot if the weather was
fair. I practised over the Lynn salt marshes,

and over Nahant beach, imagining that sharp
publisher, George Putnam. I wrote my popping
off letter and sealed it, to be opened up
if. . .: Dear Dad, Hooray for the last shining
adventure. I wish I'd made it, but no crying:
it was worth it. I have no hope we'll hook
up later; if only we could. Goodbye, luck,

love, your daughter. Summer, in Newfoundland,
the Atlantic's graveyard, waiting, gray water
and silverware washing up on shore, I read
a book about the Titanic, played draw poker
with the men, winning big, till the weather
lightened: was Bill too whiskeyed up to fly?
Cold shower, hot java; I give the word: go.

They gas it up, by my orders, heavy, so much
to get that seaplane to lumber out of the bay;
wing dips, and I slide toward the open hatch,
Slim catches me. At my log book, faithfully,
oil barrel, my table: It's the true rainbow,
the famous circle, in yellow: in the center's
our shadow? Long grind, the sea in wrinkles

like an elephant's back. Too rough & opaque
for me to take controls. I'm getting maid's
knee, kneeling at the window, where I soak
up beauty. Haze follows us, up in the stars.
So cold: N, horizon; S, smudge. Oh, sparkles
out the exhaust. The machine a marvel, & so
the mind. Instrument flying. 5000 now. Radio

dead, gas vanishing, engine missing. In mist,
blue shadow: is it real? Land! Stick back;
ride to the wharf in a Wales fisherman's boat.
Bill flies blind 2000 mi., is off by 1; look
in the papers: it's "Girl Crosses Atlantic."
I was 31. They can handle girl, get anxious
at woman. In 20 hrs. 40 min. I'm world famous,

and for what? I was a sack of potatoes. I
swear, next flight is on my lonesome. Absurd
parade, up Wall, in ticker tape: oh U.S.A.,
I'm a fake hero. And aviation? They grind
only 2 questions:—Were you afraid? What did
you wear? They insult me with "Lady Lindy."
Newspapers. All I want to do is air-gypsy

cross-country, zoom New York Pennsylvania
Indiana Ohio Missouri Oklahoma Texas New
Mexico Arizona California, do a 180. GP:
—32 cities have asked to see you. 1st solo
from sea to shining sea and back.—Really?
I pasted that story in my old scrapbook
of women's 1sts. I'm due, it's 5 o'clock:

KHAQQ TO LAE AT 7000 FEET AND MAKING 150 MPH

This watch, gold, waterproof, sure tick
of its movement, worn by that motorboat
pilot who disappeared into a big lake,
oh like his name, Seagrave, was fished
out and it given to me, around my wrist. . .

Our courting, all in minutes stolen, before
takeoff, coffee break at the office, after-

lecture taxi ride; that afternoon, flirting,
Chicago hotel, dozing on the one bed, waking
at dusk, stars in the skylight, his skimming,
licking, show me my body's love, uncovering
blue eyes open mouth tough nipples shivering
belly wet crack... Oh GP had grit, asking,
one winter; I said no, I don't want anything

all the time; and he kept on; proposal #6,
in a Lockheed hangar, in the engine's heat:
I nod, and pat his arm, climb in, and gas
her, roaring, wave my scarf, fly off, in late
October. The day I was a bride, I wore what
I always—school yearbook, under my picture,
"The girl in brown, who walks alone." Unsure,

I pick up a pencil, heart banging, early
morning: Dear Gyp, we've talked this over;
I have to write it down before we marry,
which I'm a fool to do, as it will shatter
my chance to work. It means so much, I waver,
and I don't have the heart to look ahead.
Don't be faithful, or ask me to, that's old

hat; be honest. Out of my way, and I yours;
and out of the world's eyes, we'll couple.
I need my own address, for sanctuary: this
is so attractive, but it's still a bridle,
and only love can make me stand. One final,
cold promise: if in a year it's not so rosy,
let me go. I'll do my best in all, give you

my skin, and secret, I guess you want. AE.
I shove the letter at him, in hopes, biting
my lips, like a schoolgirl, ah not to cry;
he nods at me, with a 1-sided smile, taking
my hand for the ceremony, fire crackling:
the civil wedding, without the word obey,
the judge reciting, that hard winter day,

in a fishing town, Connecticut, no bouquet,
ring borrowed from his ma, till death do us
part. My sister wires a gypsy blessing: May
the floods never rise to your cooking pots. . .
Over the broomstick, at 33. After the kiss,
to the judge's son:—I was saying, the army
won't back the autogyro, and so the navy—

the judge breaks in:—My best to you, Mrs.
Putnam.—I'm sticking with my name. When
my dream boat, comes home. . . Ah, it's news
on the bamboo fishing pole, our position:
he got himself a star sight, check it on
the flight chart; great: my dreams no more
will roam. On course: radio back to shore.

KHAQQ TO LAE POSITION LATITUDE 4º 33.5'
SOUTH LONGITUDE 159º 7' EAST

If she offers her body, and he his money,
is that a marriage of spirits? Man, look
at a woman and see her, human; if she
says I, it's better; she blooms at work.
I was exalted the day the go-for-broke
Ruth Nichols, in her stripped down Vega
and her long johns, out of Jersey City,

went for altitude at the end of winter;
and she, who'd told her big $ family
forget society girl, she was a flyer,

had no money for a real oxygen supply;
with a hose and tank, she whirls away
in the sky going dark and darker blue,
over 5 miles, and breathing below zero

air into her mouth, till her last gallons
are out, she plunges, her eardrums in pain,
down to the airport; they ask how it was:
at 1st, she can't, her tongue is frozen. . .

I live in a shifting world, and so soon
I pack it up and go, wherever, and those
old snapshots kind of hold it in my eyes.

Like the Steichen, of the glass mural, at
Radio City, New Roxy Theater, 9 windows:
at left, dark column, cut by sprays, next
to curtains, all curling, in step designs,
and open, a stage? a woman, in her arms,
a shawl, pouring, her back to us, the sky
in ribbons, above her, lit by electricity

and mirrors; pearl light, out the window,
hint of snow, when I, mysterious, lowered
the paper, saying,—Okay with you if I fly
the Atlantic solo, in spring? He called
Balchen, with Amundsen at the north, Byrd
at the south, pole, ice seas, blue eyes:
—You're ready, with a log over 1000 hrs;

we'll fix the ship up with a 500 hp super-
charged engine. She looks over the thick
skyscrapers, at the wind in strips of air
laced by energy lines, white rainbow in back
of the airplane, as if thinking—I'm stuck
in an office, grime windows, a crack of sky:
you fly for me, Amelia. She sees the Vega,

star bright, over the waves, blue curving,
green straight, double; propeller whirls,
energy circles; black sections, looming
rain; in the off geometry, hard showers.
We'd asked what's it like out, what does
Doc Kimball say? Earth turns, the weather

blows east across it, like water counter-

clockwise, haunting him, inside his bureau,
in thin telegrams, at his desk, building
a map of isobars, and the mid-Atlantic low.
One last look at the dogwoods, blossoming,
and out to Harbour Grace; the man pumping
gas:—Good luck, Miss Earhart.—I can use
it; 7 women have died trying.—You choose

this anniversary of Lindbergh?—Oh, I did;
5 years: the tide comes in and out, and we
edge into the miraculous, so maybe your kid
can walk on the moon, Major Aldrin. I eye
old Balchen, with a little smile:—Think I
can make it?—Yeah, sure. I sit in the red
airplane, rev it, check the mags, and nod.

KHAQQ TO LAE ON COURSE FOR HOWLAND ISLAND
ALTITUDE 12000 FEET CHANGING FROM 6210 TO 3105

LAE TO KHAQQ STAY ON THIS FREQUENCY SIGNAL WEAK
HEAVY STATIC

KHAQQ TO LAE WISH TO CONTACT AMERICAN CUTTER
ON THE NIGHT BAND

Into the wind, and the long sundown, so I
won't arrive at dusk on an unknown coast,
with my lucky elephant bracelet and a saw-
buck, oh out to sea, beauty, action, just
for that, and to show a woman can, I start;
between the private takeoff and the shock
of landing, there's no witness to my work.

4 hrs out, lightning, and I see the moon
blink, the altimeter, hands swinging, ah!
out of commission, the rain blowing down,
and I see fire, in the manifold ring—why

did I look? Wasn't the storm south; am I
off course? That crack is worse; the weld
is broken; if it splits . . . Well, should

I go back? Night landing, Newfoundland,
heavy fuel; in 4 hrs I'll be half-way . . .
Zero visibility, no horizon, burning, and
I shove on, climb over the clouds, now
I ice up, I'm spinning, dirty window,
god! but Lindbergh, same trouble, and he
made it: I go down to melt, till I see

whitecaps breaking, on the black tide,
glad it's not a smooth sea, wave salts
under my nose, manifold shaking; I hold
under ice, over water, sip tomato juice,
in steady mist, too low, no instruments,
where is the plane, in space? The gyro
compass, a life-saver. 1st light, I fly

white clouds, foam blowing, north, west,
ice on the wing's edge, the sun dazzling,
dark glasses, did I drift south? East,
skim water, to a boat, manifold rattling,
I switch to reserve tanks, gauge leaking
on me, and what if the fumes catch fire?
Don't miss the island; I can't see far . . .

KHAQQ TO ITASCA DO YOU READ ME A SHIP
IN SIGHT AHEAD

It's Ireland, turn right, into the high
hills, thunder, and no altimeter, I 180,
up a railroad, hope for a city, no, only
a sloping farm, cows scare, I light, oh
in the grass, the manifold in flames, so
tired, the engine, unfailing, the heart,
and I sit in the cockpit: I've done it.

—Where am I?—In Gallagher's pasture.
Come far?—From America.—Are you man
or woman?—Could I have a sip of water?
GP, on the phone:—Oh, your voice again,
AE, you are the world's greatest woman.
—I was on fire, and I figured, you know,
I'd rather drown than burn, so I flew low.

Our trans-Atlantic talk, green headland,
lighthouse, shamrock, leaves in a fan
with a crazy flower, and water, down and
into a blue pool signed: Maurice Heaton;
under the mural, with my legs up, I lean
on my hand, natural smile, eyes, not shy,
downcast: I look straight into the camera.

The Irish taxed me, for importing gas,
the Lindberghs, in mourning, telegraphed,
Smith, who I beat to it, was gracious,
the mobs . . . I will meet you, I will greet
you, London Paris Rome Washington, out
to touch me; newspapers:—It's unwomanly.
—There is no woman, but women, and we

are what we do. All the aeronautical prizes:
the Distinguished Flying Cross, 1st woman,
from Congress, and I don't know, silver wings
of the 381st National Observation Squadron,
American Society British Guild French Legion;
I stuck songs and praise in a folder, Bunk;
with Eleanor Roosevelt, I did the cakewalk,

we went flying. I met Orville:—Well, did
you know there was a Wright sister? Back
when, she was a schoolteacher; her hard
money it was that let Wilbur and I work;
she sewed the wings for us at Kitty Hawk.
And I saw Babe Didrikson air the javelin
and win, at the Olympics, and took off in

my little red bus, non-stop record 19 hrs,
only 1 minute over Hawks, cross-country.

One winter day, kicking Hollywood ideas
around:—I like Kate Hepburn cast as me,
but I still want to solo the Pacific; oh
I know it's killed 10. Hawaii businessmen
backed me, to advertise their island sun.

The navy said no till we upped the radio's
range, and the Star Bulletin was uneasy I'd
sold out for 10 grand, to sugar and hotels:
the boys were about to fold; I up and said:
—I smell cowardice in here. I'll go ahead
with or without your bankroll. They clapped.
I gave Gyp a popping off letter:—I'll lift

that heavy load, off a rough field, as best
I can, and if I don't shine this time, it
won't be because the engine isn't excellent
or women can't fly. All night, breaking out
the window, the waves, lagging and constant,
not sleeping, I was thinking of the captain
last November, who went down in that ocean:

1 weak sos, and he was gone; and dreaming
of Ruth Law, and that day in 1916 Chicago
she was out to top a man: she's shimmying
through the Loop, and out to open country,
with a clock and compass, in a wheelbarrow
with wings, the end, rocking the last drops
into the carb, and gliding to a distance

record; down in the barnyard, she answers
—What? Oh I did it for nothing, just to
do it. The tropic rain, all morning, is
slackening at last: that field is muddy,

wind against me, but, storms on the way,
it's this afternoon or never. I see news-
reels, ambulances, fire trucks, and ladies

with handkerchiefs, ready for an emergency:
I roll, wheels in mud, spraying, get light,
and look, my old mechanic, running with me;
I side-to-side, and into the air, I jolt,
all of a sudden, drop, don't crash, ignite
the extra fuel, full power and she catches,
oh I'm this machine. Over the cane fields,

I swing out toward Diamond Head, and round
the point, gray sky; they going to shoot
at me, too low over the navy yard? in scud
to 6K and above, stars, my god, rising out
of the ocean, hang outside of the cockpit:
I fly out of the Magellanic Clouds, slide
under Polaris toward morning, the mainland.

14 changes in course, by my little chart,
the big ocean: will I see, ah searchlight;
I blink my lights 3 times; like buckshot,
their code, crackling. I radio back, not
my position, but the filmy clouds, washed
out moon, the black water, in come-and-go
drizzle blowing in through the port window.

I drink hot chocolate, and interview live
on the all-night talk show, stand still,
in rapture, at the river of stars: I give
up the day-to-day for this holy dazzle.
Light at the horizon, and the lights fail
in the overwhelming sun; and what is it,
coming up too far south, by my fool chart.

No earth, white mist, I'm in my own world,
with opera in waves on the radio, crashing;
oh the last hour's hard, looking the cloud

shadows into islands, shores, dissolving;
through holes, I see blue water, rippling,
dive down, and it's a $ Liner; I can follow
her wake a ways, to the hills of California.

After Atlantic war, Pacific peace: the 1st
person to cross that ocean, and at Oakland:
—Your transmission: I'm tired?—You missed
my meaning in static: of the fog, I said.
10000 hurrah, crying, by the armed guard,
shove American Beauty roses at my breast.
That landing is in the diary of my heart.

I saw a little white horse at the circus,
and here I am, jumping through this hoop:
I record, and lecture, circle for the box
office, women in flying, till I can loop
back up. After the newsreel smiles, I slip
off to the whatever hotel, where I have
to type up the big money Times exclusive,

then out on tour, booked by my P. T. Bar-
num impresario, manager and shadow, down-
to-earth man and high-flying woman, star
of this sideshow, I blow in, 1 hr alone,
and face-to-face with that old question:
What did I wear? Come on; my flying clothes:
high laced boots, brown broadcloth britches,

white silk shirt, wild tie, drab sweater,
long leather coat, with pockets, collar,
cream silk scarf, goggles, thin leather
flying helmet; on routine flights I wear
my everydays. I'm tall as you in the air,
as light, as strong; on earth, 5'8, 117.
My hair is combed by wind, and my skin sun-

freckled; I go for the simple, clothes
that last, in grace: I design long-line
plain get-ups, not for the stay-at-home,
but the woman in motion. I go around in
pants, like nobody, ha! I'm a man woman:
I might put on overalls and carry roses,
and I'm a pilot with a string of pearls.

Ah well, not too much profit in a shirt
made of a parachute... Next: Was I scared?

I looked at the chance of dying, straight
on, and then put it out of my hard head.
If you want brave, those '29 flyers had
insides, 1st woman's air race, California
to the Ohio finish line, and the mockery

we faced: Will Rogers called it the Powder
Puff Derby, and us Sweethearts of the Air,
anything but pilots. The NAA didn't dare
let us cross the Rockies, were asking for
men as navigators, and I wouldn't enter
till they backed down. We had Ruth Elder,
ocean fighter, Phoebe Omlie, sky diver

and flying teacher, Pancho Barnes, stunt
pilot, Ruth Nichols, distance, Gladys O'
Donnell, circuit racer, and Bobbi Trout,
endurance champ, and Louise Thaden, who
held the records. Women are weak, they say,
but look at Maggie Perry, able to fly 48
hrs with typhoid; they say hysterical, but

look at Blanche Noyes, down in the mesquite,
on fire, with handfuls of sand, and at it
in the air again; they say frivolous, but
oh, look at Marvel Crosson, who bailed out
in the Gila River hills, and died wrapped
in her parachute silk, for love of flight. . .
Okay, I'll ask you: Who's Lady Lindy? Not

me: no lady, not Lindbergh. Newspapermen
are fish for the old lure of alliteration
and hook of categories. I crossed my own
Atlantic, and my name is Earhart.—Anne,
I said,—I'm sorry; at our Rye mansion,
under the dogwoods, and she with her blue
questioning eyes, possible smile,—You

are tall and slim, true face, cool eyes,

clear mind, in balance, and bolt across
oceans... Ah, but the country headlines
my act, margins it, and back to business.
Aviation pays women 38¢/hr, and men 70¢,
for the same job; I asked a manager why:
—They work for less; my costs are high...

Because of the accident of sex, a woman
has to do it better, for the same credit.
They don't trust us with a real airplane,
think our periods make us crazy; I asked
a circus lady if she excused her tight-
rope walkers:—Oh no, for heaven's sakes!
I campaigned for 2 years, at Air Commerce;

at last, they hired 1 woman, as a token.
I'm afraid all my 1sts add up to zero,
women pilots, blackballed, by power men:
I opened the door for the stewardess. Oh,
I say go ahead, against the odds, fly;
I'm here to sway girls: you can do it
if, like grandma said, you have spirit;

I'm proof: ignore old boys, don't take no
for an answer; how can you earn your spurs
if you don't ride? make it happen. The day
we're equals in the sun will be centuries
in coming. Good night. I walk in applause,
to the loose reception, and sign my little
autograph, talk to the local paper, till

midnight, I'm on the road, to Sioux City,
300 miles. I stack the money up from books
like The Fun of It: Random Records of My
Own Flying and Women in Aviation, stamps,
advertising, handouts, whatever it takes
for the next flight. And go to sleep: hold
you closely, my own... I'm looking to land

on an atoll in the lonesome Pacific: ah
women, what is harder? Well, it's after
12, in the crescent moon, and no radio
from the navy cutter, flying over water
in the dark, again. I wish I could hear
sign on, swing music, and any old shows,
human voices, chattering, over the noise

of engines, but no contact yet, too far.

After the 2nd ocean, FDR:—You're a woman
from pioneer America, out on the frontier
of air, and showed flying isn't for men
only. I founded the 99s, for all women
pilots and aerial experience. . . Invited
to Mexico: Wiley Post, around-the-world

air man, with the eye patch:—What route?
—Straight as I can.—Across the Gulf?
—Yeah.—Kind of far; how much time cut?
—1 hr.—Amelia, don't; it isn't safe.
—Hah, I can hardly wait: I had to laugh.
I go by midnight, in the generous moon,
over Baja, white haze, white water, on

1 engine, overheating, over the sierra,
to the high mesa; I'd drift out of line,
they said, last leg: I find Guadalajara,
this unknown railroad, grain of sand in
my eye and the maps blurred, and I sit down,
dry lake, sign language with the vaqueros,
who know me; they motion south, and I rise.

Why am I a chalkboard on which they love
to scrawl adjectives? They call me simple,
complex, thorough, grand, pioneer, above
my age, ahead of my time, unique, immortal,
restless, rebelling, strong, original,
calm, invulnerable, open-air, slow-moving,
speed-crazy, on wings, upward, dazzling,

unexpectedly feminine, quiet, music- and
book-loving, intellectual, fire-eating,
quick, honest, fascinating, fascinated,

valid, dreaming, down-to-earth, searching,
foresighted, illegible, mysterious, caring,
misunderstood, misunderstanding, graceful,
steady, in style, inspiring, practical,

excellent, imperfect, lucky, many-sided,
equal, skilled, in charge, free-spirited,
supporting, rival, devoted, open-handed,
flush, hard up, moving, tender-hearted,
cool, poised, light, fun, high-minded,
scared, brave, daring, elegant, comely,
arrogant, famous, solitary, friendly,

loved, gold-digging, gracious, well-bred,
rude, praiseworthy, praised, human, humane,
pure, home-wrecking, sacrificing, tousled,
legendary, childless, magical, uncertain,
unorthodox, undaunted, undefeated, uncommon,
undomestic, unfailing, ungracious, unfaithful,
unbound, unsentimental, untiring, unusual,

tomboy, golden girl, true daughter, dear
sister, nurse, pacifist, horseback rider,
student, clerk, photographer, truck driver,
social worker, pilot, wife, loner, author,
talker, feminist, designer, record holder,
hero, the 1st lady of the American sky:
a cloud of language, through which I fly.

Oh the horses of Mexico, and hat dancing
with the charros, and women will be free
as men are, whatever country, I'm hoping;
the army boys lay out a 3-mile runway
on the Lake Texcoco mud flats, warn me
she won't go up in the rare air; I'm in,
check by headlights, and the young moon.

I push her past 100 mph, and in 1 mile she
rises, up over the bull ring, the mud

ranchos, the floating gardens, Xochimilco,
the snows of Popocatapetl, and the divide,
clouds down... Moon and water—I go around
thunderheads—will sing... lit up by pure
lightning; my ship's handsome, nobody here

to see. Blue gulf, last flight in a single
engine, on to New Orleans, I pick up radio,
slide home on that party line, to Mobile;
my partner in the east coast shuttle:—Hey,
that's enough, Amelia; better land; and I,
—No thanks, I'm going on; at the hangar,
in the mob, cops yank me in a tug-of-war.

KHAQQ TO ITASCA 14 HOURS OUT CLOUDY AND OVERCAST DO YOU READ ME

I wonder if they'll pick that up in static.
This flight got under way at a forum: Women
and the Changing World, for the Herald, N.Y.,
Wiley's airplane down with Will:—I'm not in
the lost generation; it's okay to rally on
peace, dance to low-down jazz, look cubist,
fly if it's in their hearts. This president

invited me to work his coeds up toward
careers, and that Indiana research outfit
poured in 40 grand to get me a Lockheed
Electra, S3H-1 Wasp engines, 1100 hp at
full, on my birthday 39; shakedown flight,
I thought, "I'll put a girdle round about
the earth:" Shakespeare, dreaming; and not

at high latitude, in the short cut, but
at the world's waist, across the 7 heavens
in my own Golden Hind, 1 more long flight
in me. Oh charts are fine: the compass rose,
the courses, changes, the prevailing winds,
distances, notes on local weather, main
altitudes, crisis landings. . . white ocean.

Call it world flight, and I have 5 chapters
and 1001 details to Scheherezade through:
get money, lay out headings, arrange visas,
line up fuel drums, mortgage my future, ah
but what are futures for? I study zero
visibility flying, fish for a star navigator,
and reel him in, off of a South Seas clipper,

Fred Noonan, old hand, 1-time hard drinker,
to handle the chronometers, bubble sextant,
pelorus, aperiodic compass, drift indicator,
and back over the catwalk from this cockpit.
Jackie Cochran, ace flyer, and I heart-
to-heart over aviation all Xmas, and she
opens me up to the 6th sense, telepathy:

United Airlines flight was missing,—Here,
I prophesy, and touch the map's pale color,
telephone, and the wreck's under my finger.
She sees I'm crossing over uncharted water,
and worries; we promise to esp each other.
In the blue winter dusk, the traffic light,
I see this old man, going hungry, and not

begging: I tell Gyp, so hard, I'd hate it,
I don't think I'll live to be old. . . I fly
off on St. Patrick's, dip under the almost
done Golden Gate, and sight a plane at sea,
right engine in and out, ice in carb, I
leaned it too much, rainbow, gold nothing
sun down, copilot on, and Venus setting.

KHAQQ TO ITASCA BROADCAST ON 3105 KCS ON
HOUR AND HALF OVERCAST

I'm back on instruments, the moon's a life-
saver, giving us horizon; they're shooting
star sights out of the hatch, through brief
holes in the clouds; at last, stars fading,
I throttle down to arrive in the morning,
keeping it at 10° to the starboard bow,
and set a trans-Pacific record anyhow.

After a test flight, right propellers had
conked out, I taxi down the even pavement
at Oahu, our destination, Howland Island,
into a slight crosswind, 1000 ft, the right

wing sags, shocks gone? power down left,
it's swerving, no control, ground loop, ah
slam down, white sparks up from the belly,

our ship, dripping with fuel, time slows
to a still point, the airfield sliding,
fingers uncurling, I—remember wheels
stuck in the mud, tall grass, she noses
over, the safety belt breaks, my body's
sailing, to the dry weeds, the airplane
on its back; that morning, in a bad spin,

I hit the brakes, leaning, the door opens
and knocks me in, and my skull's cut; okay,
I crash, like anybody: the vulgar papers
and movies are bored to death, can't do
without crack-ups and lost flyers, but ah,
that isn't aviation. If I don't come back,
I'll go down a legend my ghost will mock:

yeah, it was a woman who died, not a man—
so what? 1st time, I was flying back
from the Goodyear field: if I go in low,
I'll hit the eucalyptus trees that flank
the runway, so I pull up, stall, pancake
into a cabbage patch, bite tongue, fingers,
like now, uncurling, I—cut the switches:

if I don't burn up, I'm trying it again.
It's a miracle; heaven, it hurts to see,
out of my daze, that fabulous airplane
broken... of the tender love I bring. I
sigh:—We'll go on around the other way.
4 a.m., when the birds tweet, and I radio
my waves ahead, toward the light of day.

KHAQQ TO ITASCA CAN'T HEAR YOU ON 3105 KCS
PARTLY CLOUDY

Questions come up:—Why on earth are you
going ahead?—Oh, are you saying my luck
will run out, like front money, that how
it works? I'm just this way; I jaywalk
where my heart leans, and risk is music.
It's useless, like poetry, this gesture:
I light out into the wilderness of air,

and to validate a dream in a woman's eye.
All my pals at the airfield say pull out;
Louise, on that last night:—You're crazy;
you're tops, now and always, nothing to get
and all to lose, why open up to a knock-out?
I shake my head as we sit on the life raft:
—Ha, you should talk; didn't you fly that

air race with a gas tank around your neck?
I've gone all out, and so this is my fling.
Ah, my date's already in the doomsday book,
when I'm done; if I go down, it's doing
what I love. The off-shore breeze blowing
in my hair:—I never run. My one regret,
no time to have a kid, like yours; just

tell her to ride that iron horse, ah build
harbor bridges, and go after the bad guys.
That sugar daddy, Baruch, gave 25 grand:
—I like your everlasting guts. . . I buzz
5th Ave. at noon, to advertise, tip wings
at 42nd St.; and I sprawl, grease monkey,
watching it get better, navigation, radio,

load. . . Kind of tired: pull out that can,
tomato juice, ice pick. We pack by stars,

land compass, matchbox, little ax, canteen,
life boat, flare pistol, orange kite, rags,
good night, dear pony, and I rub her nose.
Dark out, in the a.m., and the human city
asleep, crew yawning, and the air heavy

with dew, so fine for wings to cut into,
the engines idling, and the quick goodbyes,
coffee, and into the tight cockpit, stow
bag and bottle, oh the feeling, 50 dials,
green magic, flight plan, it's in my hands,
I'm up to getaway speed, without a word,
we're in the air, May 20, out of Oakland.

It's all a whirl, the country abstracting,
actual oaks, and shadow trees, I sky down
to Burbank, Tucson, saguaros, sand blowing,
New Orleans, old night, riverboat, jazz in
the air, Miami, lunch at the greasy spoon
across the coast highway, oh the buttermilk,
the lighthouse, over the shoals, the Tropic,

San Juan, white church, in the Gulf Stream,
Caripito, red roofs, oil tanks, orchids,
grapes, Paramaribo, at the edge, steam
on the river, jungle, leopard, Fortaleza,
tidal flats, modern towers, catamarans,
baskets of fish, Natal, red dirt, ibis,
shipwreck under ribbons of surf, across

the Atlantic rains, to St. Louis, thick
cloud, oasis of palms, simple huts, Dakar,
peninsula, rose city, human smells, mosaic,
Gao, queen, pyramid in ruins, mosque, poor
barrens, Ft. Lamy, blank space, El Fasher,
thorn hedge, sultan's palace, rush baskets,
Khartoum, heat waves, squares and streets

the imperial flag, camel rider, old Nile,

Massawa, sailboat on the Red Sea, salt
piles, Assab, empty coast, bone dry well,
forbidden Arabia, border, Karachi, desert
ship, Calcutta, aerodrome, black eagles,
crowded harbor, city, elephant and howdah,
Akyab, banyan, solid monsoon, mud volcano,

Rangoon, flying fish, gold pagoda, quick
rickshaws, Bangkok, temples, junks, dream
waters, Singapore, island, theater music,
Bandoeng, rice terraces, shadow drama,
Surabaya, dog cart, Koepang, pleasure dome,
dry grass, cliffs, last outpost, merchant,
green seas, Port Darwin, kangaroo, forest,

pearl diver, Lae, village in river, monkey,
oh, hallelujah motion, around the world.
Backfire and fire, cross the equator, no
Neptune to douse me, wrong turn, long ride,
back track; and now, over the dateline, led
on by the horizon, to yesterday, skywriting. . .
Air speed, time, distance, the true heading:

KHAQQ TO ITASCA WANT BEARING ON 3105 ON HOUR
WILL WHISTLE IN MIKE ABOUT 200 MILES OUT
APPROXIMATELY WHISTLING NOW

Whoo; wait for answer. . . And in this other
world all the way, this melting geography:
through the rain maker, low sheet, thunder-
head, fair-weather, snail clouds, and into
the mackerel sky, white veil, sun's halo,
up to ice crystals, mare's tail, anvil;
I rode Antony's horse, and Hamlet's whale,

slammed into hills, into oceans of haze,
invisible stream, no map, no buoy, flows
from high to low, and easterly, over waves
of heat, slow rocking, updrafts like sprays,

rough air, or easy sailing, and heaven is
the troposphere... We'll be sweethearts, oh
forever... Old earth lies in squares below,

like stanzas... I can't raise them, no
receiver, dynamo working under the seat;
I'll relay it to him, in back: bad radio...

The east is lightening, and with no rest,
morning is close; this signal, this ghost
transmission, will fade out; I'll sag into
black ocean, abide, swaying in the agony

of the tides, which won't give up the dead.
Ah quick, little to tell; after this wave,
last words, grace me, now and then, rolled
in the mystery, with a moment of your love. . .
Time's flying, quarter to 7; if I can give
them my voice to follow, and get a bearing,
we'll close on that island in not too long,

by his star fix, out of the all night rack,
and the sun glaring on the colossal water.

KHAQQ TO ITASCA PLEASE TAKE BEARING ON US
AND REPORT IN 1/2 HOUR I WILL MAKE NOISE
IN MIKE ABOUT 100 MILES OUT

Day off, we forded the river in a truck
to a cocoanut grove, huts on stilts, fire
of the women, oh the jungle to explore,
and back to cable a chapter to the Herald:
We won't be home by 4th of July as hoped.

I was looking west, over Pacific breakers,
and this last evening, east; in a few days,
the world's river's run under us, the end's
this ocean; I'll be glad, its blue hazards
behind me. But in my old poem, "Courage is
the price that life exacts for granting peace.
The soul that knows it not knows no release. . ."

At every landing, passports, visas, all
those countries, and 1 sky: and America
ahead, good times, hard times, dust bowl,
new deal, steel strikes, gun men, jumbo
circus, and coast-to-coast flights daily,
sliding toward war... Why is that island
How Land? Low reef, mile long, 1/2 wide;

but I'm Air Heart. I let her down, don't
see the cutter, ah, only acres of water,
the dazzle at the equator, did we drift
north, arrow to the left, on the gas meter,
from head winds, carb, the sun line's where?

KHAQQ CALLING ITASCA WE MUST BE ON YOU BUT
CAN'T SEE YOU GAS IS RUNNING LOW BEEN UNABLE
TO REACH YOU BY RADIO FLYING AT 1000 FEET

I ain't lost but I don't know where I'm at,
as the old barnstormer said: what was it,

his fixes, or the charts, not enough fuel
for other islands, we need to stretch it,
maximum cruise, go down to 1 1/2 stall,
on the back side of the power curve, point
up, overshoot, turn south on the current
line of position run forward from the last
star, and circle, in hopes we make it out.

KHAQQ CALLING ITASCA WE ARE CIRCLING BUT
CAN'T HEAR YOU GO AHEAD ON 7500 WITH A
LONG COUNT NOW OR ON THE SCHEDULED TIME
ON THE 1/2 HOUR

Come on, give me the letter A, like you...

DOT DASH DOT DASH DOT DASH DOT DASH DOT DASH
GO AHEAD ON 3105

Oh, the coast guard! if the direction loop
homes on that frequency, we'll read them now:

KHAQQ CALLING ITASCA WE RECEIVED YOUR SIGNALS
BUT CAN'T GET A MINIMUM PLEASE TAKE BEARING
ON US AND ANSWER ON 3105 WITH VOICE
DOT DASH DOT DASH DOT DASH DOT DASH DOT DASH

Around the circle, bad omens, as I slip:
this route never flown; and on her lit up
globe, mama couldn't see the island; for
weight I left my lucky bracelet back there;

I didn't wear my wings, on this one flight.
Smooth air, sure of our longitude, ceiling
unlimited, ah but no position, poor contact:
if we go in. . . oh Gyp! I was a kid, reading
in our library, and in all the showboating
adventure books, they had none with girl
heroes, and I—well, maybe now they will.

KHAQQ TO ITASCA WE ARE ON THE LINE 157 337
NORTH AND SOUTH WILL REPEAT MESSAGE WE WILL
REPEAT THIS ON 6210 KCS WAIT 3105 WE ARE
RUNNING ON LINE LISTEN 6210 KCS

It's a dead stick landing, and the tail's
down, lessen the blow. When my dream boat
comes home. . . Ditch in the 6 foot waves.
We've come 24000 miles. Oh, that was it,
I was thinking, yesterday, on my way out
to the aerodrome: Charlie let us play in
the old 2-seat carriage in grandma's barn,

with an invisible horse, the blue pigeon,
the girls, and I, whooping at dangers in
the clouds of dust, imaginary country, on
the way to Cherryville, never arriving. In
the salty morning, I know what's on the line,

but la-de-da; in the come what may sun,
I go on walking out to the lovely airplane.

Sources

1
The Fun of It. Amelia Earhart, 1932
Last Flight. Amelia Earhart, 1937
Letters from Amelia. Amelia Earhart, edited by Jean Backus, 1982
Amelia: Pilot in Pearls. Edited by Shirley Dobson Gilroy, 1985 (autographed)
Amelia, My Courageous Sister. Muriel Earhart Morrissey and Carol Osborne, 1987
Still Missing: Amelia Earhart and the Search for Modern Feminism. Susan Ware, 1993

2
20 Hrs. 40 Min. Amelia Earhart, 1928
Life. July, 1937
Soaring Wings. George Putnam, 1939
Daughter of the Sky. Paul Briand, 1960
The Search for Amelia Earhart. Fred Goerner, 1966
Winged Legend. John Burke, 1970
Amelia Earhart Lives. Joe Klaas, 1970
Women Aloft. Valerie Moolman, 1981
Amelia Earhart: The Final Story. Vincent Loomis and Jeffrey Ethell, 1985
Eyewitness: The Amelia Earhart Incident. Thomas Devine, 1987
Lost Star. Patricia Lauber, 1988
Amelia Earhart: What Really Happened at Howland. George Carrington, 1989
The Sound of Wings. Mary Lovell, 1989
Amelia Earhart. Richard Tames, 1989
Amelia Earhart: Challenging the Skies. Susan Sloate, 1990
Amelia Earhart: Courage in the Sky. Mona Kerby, 1990
Life. April, 1992
Biography: Amelia Earhart. Produced by Jack Haley, 1992
The Search for Amelia Earhart. Produced by H. Thomas Jones, 1992
The American Experience: Amelia Earhart. Produced by Nancy Potter, 1993
"Love of Flying." *The First Anthology.* Gore Vidal, edited by Robert Silvers and others, 1993

3

Richard III. V.iii; Hamlet. IV.vii; A Midsummer Night's Dream. III.ii, II.i.
   William Shakespeare, 1623
Rubaiyat of Omar Khayyam of Naishapur, 44. Edward Fitzgerald, 1879
The Wonderful Wizard of Oz. L. Frank Baum, 1900
"Zone." *Alcools.* Guillaume Apollinaire, 1913
"When My Dream Boat Comes Home." Cliff Friend and Dave Franklin, 1937
Wind, Sand and Stars. Antoine de Sainte-Exupery, 1939
The Student Pilot's Flight Manual. William Kershner, 1990
Asia/Pacific. Hong Kong Standard. www.hkstandard.com, 7/24/96
Weather Forecast for Local Aviation. Royal Observatory. www.info.gov.hk/ro, 7/24/96

4

The Complaint of Rosamond. Samuel Daniel, 1592
Folklore of Shakespeare. F. F. Dyer, 1883
The Second Sex. Simone de Beauvoir, 1949
"The Airplane." *Jazz.* Henri Matisse, 1947
Elizabethan Poetry. Hallet Smith, 1952
This Fabulous Century: 1930-1940. Edited by Ezra Bowen, 1969
Rhyme and Meaning in the Poetry of Yeats. Marjorie Perloff, 1970
"Introduction to The Rape of Lucrece." *The Riverside Shakespeare.* Hallet Smith, 1974
Ghosts. Tim Appenzeller and David Thomson, 1984
Passport to World Band Radio. Edited by Lawrence Magne, 1990
Kids Discover Weather. Edited by Stephen Brewer, 1994

Larry Beckett's poetry ranges from brief lyrics and songs to blank sonnets and hundred-page narrative works. Song to the Siren, written with Tim Buckley, has been recorded by This Mortal Coil, Robert Plant, Diana Trimble, John Frusciante, Sinead O'Connor, Bryan Ferry, Alfie Boe, George Michael, Dead Can Dance, Jann Klose, and Stuart Anthony. His sonnets and madrigals center on marriage day-to-day, with music and intensity: they were published in *Songs and Sonnets* by Rainy Day Women Press. *Beat Poetry*, a study of the poets and poetry of the fifties San Francisco renaissance, was published by Beatdom Books. His epic *American Cycle*, inspired by our history and legends, includes *Paul Bunyan*, from Smokestack Books, *Wyatt Earp*, forthcoming from Alternating Current Press, and *Amelia Earhart*.

www.ingramcontent.com/pod-product-compliance
Lightning Source LLC
Chambersburg PA
CBHW070551090426
42735CB00013B/3148